Watch Out! The King is Coming

A collection of poems for personal and congregational devotions

Ian Caveen

Illustrated by Helen Pattison

O&U
Onwards & Upwards

Onwards and Upwards Publishers

4 The Old Smithy
London Road
Rockbeare
EX5 2EA
United Kingdom
www.onwardsandupwards.org

Copyright © Ian Caveen 2022

The moral right of Ian Caveen to be identified as the author of this work has been asserted by the author in accordance with the Copyright, Designs and Patents Act 1988.

All rights reserved.

No part of this publication may be reproduced or transmitted in any form or by any means, electronic or mechanical, including photocopy, recording or any information storage and retrieval system, without permission in writing from the author or publisher.

First edition, published in the United Kingdom by Onwards and Upwards Publishers Ltd. (2022).

ISBN: 978-1-78815-992-0
Illustrations: © Helen Pattison
Typeface: Sabon LT

The views and opinions expressed in this book are the author's own, and do not necessarily represent the views and opinions of Onwards and Upwards Publishers or its staff.

Unless otherwise specified, Scripture quotations are taken from the Holy Bible, New International Version® Anglicized, NIV® Copyright © 1979, 1984, 2011 by Biblica, Inc.® Used by permission. All rights reserved worldwide.

Scripture quotations marked (RSV) are from the Revised Standard Version of the Bible, copyright © 1946, 1952, and 1971 the Division of Christian Education of the National Council of the Churches of Christ in the United States of America. Used by permission. All rights reserved.

Endorsements

I have known Ian for over 20 years, and heard and read his poems during that period. When I became a Supernumerary Minister in 2006, I sat under Ian's preaching on a number of occasions and have heard him use his poems as songs, accompanying himself on the guitar (sadly because of the advance of Parkinson's, he is no longer able to do that). I believe that his work is inspired by the Holy Spirit and will be upbuilding for preachers, Christians and those seeking their way to faith. I thoroughly endorse this book and trust that many will be blessed through its words – including Ian's own testimony which it contains.

Rev. John C. Trevenna
Supernumerary Methodist Minister

This collection of poems and reflections emerges from a lifetime of Christian faith by a man immersed in the scriptures. The tone is worshipful, addressing God with delight, joy and a desire to worship and serve. There is much that will encourage individual readers, as well as material to use in public worship. It is carefully arranged around the Christian Year and its major themes, enhanced by simple, beautiful art work. When you read the story of Ian's faith in the final section, you will see where the poetry has its deep roots.

Rev. Dr Roger L. Walton
President of the Methodist Conference, 2016-17

Acknowledgements

I am grateful for the encouragement I have received from the AWE singers and worship band, West Ardsley Methodist Church (my church family); Rev. John and Eileen Trevenna; Rev. Nick and Kathryn Cutts; and my wife, Pam.

Dedicated to Paul Cadman
(1957-2022)

a close family friend who died while I was compiling this book of poems

Brothers and sisters, we do not want you to be uninformed about those who sleep in death, so that you do not grieve like the rest of mankind, who have no hope. For we believe that Jesus died and rose again, and so we believe that God will bring with Jesus those who have fallen asleep in him. According to the Lord's word, we tell you that we who are still alive, who are left until the coming of the Lord, will certainly not precede those who have fallen asleep. For the Lord himself will come down from heaven, with a loud command, with the voice of the archangel and with the trumpet call of God, and the dead in Christ will rise first.

1 Thessalonians 4:13-16

About the Author

Originally from Chester, Ian Caveen became a Christian while studying architecture at Sheffield University, through the ministry of the Navigators[1]. He met his wife, Pam, when worshipping at Christ Church, Fulwood, Sheffield, where they were married in 1980. He graduated the same year, obtaining an MA, and started his professional career working in Oldham, Greater Manchester. He and Pam moved to St Bees, Cumbria, in 1985, where their two sons were born. Since 1988, East Ardsley, Wakefield has been their home.

Ian's song-writing started in 1990 when he found himself out of work. This then developed into poetry when he was diagnosed with Parkinson's disease in 2017. Due to his Parkinson's, Ian took early retirement, but was invited to stay on as a consultant. The following year, he was also diagnosed with bladder cancer. Although the cancer treatment has been successful, the side effects have been debilitating. The coronavirus pandemic shutdown in 2020 finally forced him into full retirement.

Ian is currently a Local Preacher with the North Kirklees & Morley Circuit, and he and Pam are members of West Ardsley Methodist Church, where they are also involved with the AWE worship group and Messy Church.

---

[1] The Navigators are an international Christian missionary organisation centred primarily around universities. They have a strong ethos on discipling. The organisation was founded in the United States in the 1930s but came to the UK through the Billy Graham crusades in the 1950s.

Author's Preface

My collection of poems spans three decades. Looking back at my handwritten notes, some of my earlier poems were written as far back as 1990 and have gone through a long period of refinement. Although I have dabbled in song-writing since becoming a Christian in September 1973, my earlier songs have been lost in the mists of time. My poetry-writing coincided with me being unemployed in 1990, when the building industry in the United Kingdom was hit badly by a recession. At this time, a very high number of architects were out of work. I found it cathartic writing poetry, being able to focus on God and not the predicament I found myself in. Some of my poems were also written as songs to be played on the guitar, although my guitar-playing days have now been curtailed, due to the onset of Parkinson's disease.

As a Methodist Local Preacher, I have often used the poetry in services I have led. I pray you will find these poems helpful in your own expression of worship to the Lord – and maybe you could even try writing some of your own.

Ian Caveen

Illustrator's Preface

Like Ian, I am a member of West Ardsley Ebenezer Methodist Church – a wonderful church where I am able to explore my love of God. In fact, I am thankful to God every day that he guided me and my family to this church; this was over twenty years ago. We arrived at West Ardsley seemingly by mistake. Ian and the rest of the church family immediately made us feel at home.

From a young age, I have been interested in art, even pursuing it within further education and as a career, until God steered me down a different path of teacher support in a primary school. However, he has recently given me the opportunity to open this door again in my life, enjoying his wonderful creation as I depict it in watercolours. It was this resurgence, coupled with Ian's own creative zest, which helped give birth to this project, a project I am very grateful for as I get to explore my faith through the medium I love. Inspired by Ian's beautiful words, I have delved into the depths of my faith and truly found God's glory. I hope my illustrations afford you the same opportunity.

Helen Pattison

Contents

ADVENT 1
    Watch Out! He'll Come Like a Thief in the Night 3
    Heaven and Earth Renewed by Him 5
    Declare to the World God's News of Mercy and Love 7
    My Freedom is to Know the Christ 9
    Almighty God, Creator and Father 11

CHRISTMAS 13
    What Will Your Christmas Be Like? 15
    God's Gift to the World, His Beloved Son 17

CREATION 19
    Immortal God, Creator of the Universe 21
    Holy God, the Mighty Creator, I AM 22
    Father Most Holy, Maker of All We See 24
    How Can Mankind Say 26
    Wisps of Cloud Sailing a Pale Blue Sky 27
    Majestic Boats Drift Calmly By 29

LENT 31
    Grace Is the Undeserved Favour of God 33
    Long Ago the Prophets Foretold 35
    Heavenly Father, Forgive Us, We Pray 36
    Christ, the Eternal Light Who Guides Our Way 38
    Love Is… 39
    So Wide, So Deep Is Your Love for Us 40
    God Is… 42

GOOD FRIDAY 43
    Good Friday 45

EASTER 53
Despised, Rejected, Nailed to a Cross Was He 55
I Gaze upon His Cross, Love Poured Out for Me 57

PENTECOST 59
Devoted In Prayer 61

HOLY SPIRIT 63
O Life-giving Spirit 65
Holy Spirit, Come Blow on Us 66
O Spirit of the Living God 69

JESUS 71
Jesus, Jesus, I Hear Your Voice 73
Jesus Knows Everything About Me 74
You Are the Potter 77
'Turn to Me, Talk to Me and Trust Me,' You Say 78

HOLY TRINITY 79
Holy God, Creator and Father 81
God Beyond Us, We Worship You 82
God, the Creator of All We See 85
Holy, Holy, Great and Awesome Is He 86

WORSHIP 87
Holy, Holy Is the Lord 89

DEATH AND NEW LIFE 91
He Is Eternal, the First and the Last 93
We Mourn the Passing of Those We Love 96

My Faith Journey 99

Jesus was taken up before their very eyes, and a cloud hid him from their sight. They were looking intently up into the sky as he was going, when suddenly two men dressed in white stood beside them. 'Men of Galilee,' they said, 'why do you stand here looking into the sky? This same Jesus, who has been taken from you into heaven, will come back in the same way you have seen him go into heaven.'

Acts 1:9-11

For the Lord himself will come down from heaven, with a loud command, with the voice of the archangel and with the trumpet call of God, and the dead in Christ will rise first.

1 Thessalonians 4:16

Watch Out! He'll Come Like a Thief in the Night[2]

Watch out! He'll come like a thief in the night.[3]
Stay awake! Keep your lamps primed and bright,[4]
ready to see this glorious sight:
Christ claiming his realm, his by right.

Help us respond to his gospel today,
challenging hearts to trust and obey,
walking with Christ, seeking justice for all,
obedient to God's kingdom call.

Some sneer and mock, 'Will Christ ever come?'
living their lives, having great fun.
He will come, angels clearing the way.
Will we be ready on that day?

Heaven and earth renewed by him,[5]
restoring God's world, free from all sin.
The dead will rise, new life in Christ,
death defeated by his risen might!

---

[2] The imagery in this poem, taken from 1 Thessalonians 5, warns us to be ready for Christ the King's Second Coming, and is where the title of this book comes from. At the time of writing, the war in the Ukraine and the fear that it could spread into other parts of Europe is a concern, particularly for those living close to the Russian border. It shows how precarious peace is and how sudden war can erupt. We live in uncertain times. Whether it's climate change, the cost of living or the threat of war, are we prepared and ready for Christ's return? As this poem says, 'Help us be holy, caring, loving, we pray, living in readiness for that day.'
[3] 1 Thessalonians 5:1-3
[4] Matthew 25:1-13
[5] Revelation 21:1-4

Our lives that day will be open to him,
disclosing what is precious or sin.
Help us be holy, caring, loving, we pray,
living in readiness for that day.

Heaven and Earth Renewed by Him

Heaven and earth renewed by him,
restoring God's world, free from all sin.
The dead will rise, new life in Christ,
death defeated by his risen might!

O God, Creator and Father,
you've gathered us together
as your Kingdom People
to share your Good News,
and to advance your kingdom
of love, justice and peace.

In our worship and devotion,
open our minds to know your will.
Help us to obey your word.
Encourage us to remain faithful,
in readiness for your Son's return,
as we prepare for Christmas.

We come joyfully and gladly
to offer praise and adoration,
to you, Author of creation
and Divine Sustainer of all.
In the name of your Son,
accept our worship and praise.

Renew our hearts with his love.
By the power of your Spirit,
remodel us in your Son's image,
and with his risen power
enable us to be used by him
in the saving of your world.

Declare to the World God's News of Mercy and Love

Declare to the world God's news of mercy and love.
Sing out in song; cry out the Lord's name.
Salvation he brings; repent of your sins[6]
before he comes, his children to claim!
In humility we kneel,
in worship and praise.
To our Lord who heals,
our voices we raise!

Call out to the Lord; all he's made righteous and good!
Amazing love to all he has shown.
The Lord's goodness lasts forever the same.
Worship the Lord who sits on his throne.
In humility we kneel,
in worship and praise.
To our Lord who heals,
our voices we raise!

---

[6] Acts 17:30

Submit to the Lord and follow where he leads.
Before he returns, respond to his call.
With angels he comes in triumph to claim
his earthly throne, where mankind will fall.[7]
In humility we kneel,
in worship and praise.
To our Lord who heals,
our voices we raise!

All glory and praise
to our God who reigns.
All glory and praise
to our God who reigns.

---

[7] Acts 17:31

My Freedom is to Know the Christ

My freedom is to know the Christ,
God's Son, who died for me.
I, who was enslaved by sin,
cut loose, restored, set free;
renewed by God's refining fire,
commissioned by Christ the King
to spread his word throughout the world
telling all to trust and obey him.

Worship the Son
who reigns on high,
who will one day
return in glory from the sky.[8]

Our freedom is to forsake all
and follow him as our King.
Set apart, his Kingdom People,
our worship to him we bring.
Worthy is he to receive our praise,
God's holy Son who was slain.
'Halleluiah!' his people cry,
Our sins forgiven in his Son's name.

Worship the Son
who reigns on high,
who will one day
return in glory from the sky.

---

[8] Acts 1:9-11; 1 Thessalonians 4:16

Our freedom is to worship him
as believers bound in love,
different and yet unified
by God's Spirit from above;
one holy church of many races
with a message to proclaim:
of salvation, faith, hope and love
spoken in his glorious name.

Almighty God, Creator and Father

Almighty God, Creator and Father…

Advent is a time of preparation,
the countdown to celebrating
your Son's birthday.
While we may recall his coming
as a tiny baby,
in weakness and humility,
Advent also reminds us
that sometime in the future
your Son will come
in power and glory.
It's not for us to speculate
when this will be –
only you know when[9] –
but it's up to us to be prepared.

Help us, by your Holy Spirit…

to be ready for your Son's return.
He will ultimately be our judge.
He will judge all people
for their unproductive lives.[10]
True saving faith results
in a changed heart,
a spiritual and moral
transformation.

---

[9] Acts 1:7
[10] Matthew 25:14-30

Obeying your teaching,
resisting temptation,
serving,
helping others,
sharing our faith
are all signs of being productive,
fruit-bearing people for you.

Therefore, the LORD himself will give you a sign: the virgin will conceive and give birth to a son, and will call him Immanuel.

Isaiah 7:14

What Will Your Christmas Be Like?

What will your Christmas be like,
    will it be full of joy?
Will you be singing to the child,
    adoring and praising the boy?
What will your Christmas be like,
    will you worship the King?
Or will you leave him outside,
    cold, hungry, weeping?

Christ our Saviour and King.

Shops are full of costly gifts
    tempting us to buy,
while homeless beg on our streets,
    shivering under the starlit sky.
Christmas trees, reindeer, holly, Santa Claus.
    Fairy lights adorn
our streets on these cold nights,
    where God's Son was born.

Christ our Saviour and King.

People have such fun feasting,
    partying with good cheer,
ignoring the cries of God's Son,
    forgetting him for another year.
What will your Christmas be like,
    will it be full of joy?
Will you come and worship him,
    God's divine infant boy?

Christ our Saviour and King.

God's love is shown to us all,
    amazing love so divine.
This love revealed through his Son,
    seeking this cold heart of mine.
What will your Christmas be like,
    will you open your heart to him?
Or will you leave him outside,
    cold, hungry, weeping?

O come and worship him:
Christ our Saviour and King.
O come and worship him:
our King, our King, our King.

God's Gift to the World, His Beloved Son

God's gift to the world, his beloved Son.
His mother a virgin the seers foretold.[11]
Born in a stable, on straw bedding he lay,
poor and helpless; the promised Messiah of old.

Halleluiah!
Jesus our Saviour is born.

God, Creator King, lay helpless and still,
his throne a crib, his palace a stall;
conceived by God's Spirit, his destiny to die –
to die for our sins, a sacrifice for us all.

In a manger he lay; his mother stood by.
Poor shepherds came to worship the child
called Almighty God, Wonderful Counsellor,[12]
Prince of Peace; a child so meek and so mild.

Halleluiah!
Jesus our Saviour is born.

Men came from the east, so learned and wise,
to worship the boy whose star lit the sky:
God, Creator King, a poor Hebrew child,
to be rejected, for our sins crucified.

---

[11] Isaiah 7:14
[12] Isaiah 9:6

In the beginning was the Word, and the Word was with God, and the Word was God. He was with God in the beginning. Through him all things were made; without him nothing was made that has been made.

John 1:1-3

Immortal God, Creator of the Universe[13]

Immortal God, Creator of the universe,[14]
home to countless galaxies too many to measure.
Gas giants, rocky planets, worlds far and near,
creating and naming them for his sole pleasure.[15]

Almighty God, inventor of all space and time,
Maker of the atoms, tiny building blocks of life,
who formed the stars, who made the solar system,
who made Planet Earth a home fit for human life.

Creator God, whose loving hands skilfully wove
strands of DNA, his remarkable blueprint;
creating life on earth in its variety,
forming us in his image, God's divine imprint.

Unseen God, through his Son he is made visible.[16]
His Son's the Holy Word, God born in human flesh.[17]
He's the author, breath of life, divine sustainer;
it's through his revelation we see things afresh.

God gave the universe to explore in wonder,
skill to build satellites to launch and deploy,
to explore its vastness, in faith praising him,
admiring his handiwork for us to enjoy.

---

[13] This poem reflects on the beauty of God's 'good' creation and is quite fitting due to the recent launch and deployment of the James Webb telescope. The pictures of the cosmos taken by the Hubble telescope have been impressive; the Webb telescope will be a hundred times more powerful than Hubble.
[14] Genesis 1:1; Hebrews 11:3
[15] Psalm 147:4; Revelation 4:11 (KJV)
[16] Colossians 1:15
[17] John 1:14

Holy God, the Mighty Creator, I AM[18]

Holy God, the mighty Creator, I AM,[19]
who Moses met on Mount Sinai's height;[20]
righteous, immortal, the eternal God,
whose fire displayed his glory and might.

Living God, who commands the stars to shine,
who stirs the sea, so that its waves roar;[21]
Maker of all things, the awesome I AM,
we bow in worship; we praise and adore.

Give thanks to the Lord, for he is good;
his faithful love endures forever.[22]

Jesus said, 'Before Abraham was, I AM.'[23]
He orders the sea to be calm and still.[24]
He is the image of the unseen God,[25]
who was crucified on Calvary's hill.

---

[18] This poem was written around the same time as *He Is Eternal, the First and the Last*, when my father passed away in September 2013.
[19] Exodus 3:13-14
[20] Exodus 19:3
[21] Isaiah 51:15
[22] Psalm 107:1
[23] John 8:58-59
[24] Matthew 8:26
[25] Colossians 1:15

Jesus said, 'I am the true light of the world,'[26]
Saviour, Son of God,[27] the bread of life.[28]
I am the true vine,[29] redeemer and healer,
restorer and the way out of discord and strife.

Give thanks to the Lord, for he is good;
his faithful love endures forever.

Living God, who commands the stars to shine,
who stirs the sea, so that its waves roar,
Maker of all things, the awesome I AM,
we bow in worship; we praise and adore;
we bow in worship; we praise and adore
Jesus Christ our Lord.

---

[26] John 8:12
[27] John 10:36
[28] John 6:35
[29] John 15:1

Father Most Holy, Maker of All We See

Father most holy, Maker of all we see,
mighty, all-seeing, eternal is he;[30]
righteous, immortal, hidden from our eyes,[31]
vastly intelligent, all-powerful and wise.
Mortals shudder at the sound of his voice.
Myriads of angels worship and rejoice,
declaring his glory to his creation,
a symphony of praise, of loving adoration.

Father of knowledge, source of all wisdom,
your Son's the way to your holy kingdom.
His yoke is easy, his burden is light;
he's a lamp to our feet in the darkest of night.
Loving Father, your goodness is endless;
your Son is the pathway to all righteousness,
a path unreachable by effort alone –
access granted by faith; his revealed Word has shown.

---

[30] Proverbs 15:3
[31] 1 Timothy 1:17

Father of Israel, a fiery cloud night and day,
terrifying, all-consuming deity displayed.
who can stand before such a holy Being?
God, so righteous, who brings salvation and healing.
In Christ, God's Son, we stand washed in his blood,[32]
escaping God's wrath, like Noah in the flood,[33]
proclaiming, 'Whatever we gain, we count as loss,'[34]
knowing God's Son, our Saviour, by way of the cross.

---

[32] 1 John 1:7
[33] Romans 5:9
[34] Philippians 3:7-8

How Can Mankind Say

How can mankind say
that there's no Creator God;
mere mortals to theorise
creation has happened by chance?
Mankind has faith in multiverse
and string theories;
have the heavens appeared
by sheer chance?

Claiming to be wise,
mankind became foolish, unwise,[35]
exchanging the glory
of the holy, immortal God
for theories from the pages
of modern science,
bowing to the god of science,
not the Creator God.

---

[35] Romans 1:21-23

Wisps of Cloud Sailing a Pale Blue Sky [36]

Wisps of cloud sailing a pale blue sky,
tinted red, reflecting the sun.
Hills silhouetted, heathery grey
sculpted by God's creative Son.

Halleluiah! Praise to God,
Lord, Creator and our King!
We bow in worship.
Halleluiah!
Halleluiah! To Christ we sing.

Darkness descends, a white form appears,
a glistening disc of silvery light;
flickering starlight through ghostly mist
illustrating God's creative might.

The unwise in their heart say there's no God,[37]
believing all this has happened by chance!
Creation declares the glory of God.[38]
Praise him with tambourines and strings; let's dance!

Halleluiah! Praise to God,
Lord, Creator and our King!
We bow in worship.
Halleluiah!
Halleluiah! To Christ we sing.

---

[36] These verses were written while camping in the Lake District.
[37] Psalm 14:1
[38] Psalm 19:1

A gentle breeze rustles through the trees,
swaying shapes crossing a moonlit land;
an echoing cry, a hooting owl,
proclaiming God's creative hand.

Majestic Boats Drift Calmly By[39]

Majestic boats drift calmly by,
billowing sails translucent white
swaying against a pale blue sky,
its wake a wave of glistening light.

Swans and wild fowl quietly feed,
cattle graze, as boats glide by.
Birds in the tall grass eat the seed,
flocks of geese in formation fly.

Weeping willows sway in the breeze,
pink flowers litter riversides.
Gnarled branches of fallen trees
flounder in the ebbing tide.

Hulks jut out from muddy shores,
remains of long-forgotten boats.
Wherry men have withdrawn their oars,
boatmen in long waxy coats.

Dusk descends, a white mist appears
swirling wraith-like in the moonlight;
dancing shapes which feed our fears,
ghostly stories of the night.

---

[39] Written whilst on a boating holiday on the Norfolk Broads.

The Broads echo a bygone age;
wind pumps lie ruined, motionless.
History on every page,
a place of calm and eeriness.

God gave us this world to enjoy,
to praise him for his good creation,[40]
to care for and not to destroy,
awaiting creation's redemption.[41]

---

[40] Genesis 1:31
[41] Romans 8:18-22

Lent

'Even now,' declares the LORD,
'return to me with all your heart,
with fasting and weeping and mourning.'
Rend your heart
and not your garments.
Return to the LORD your God,
for he is gracious and compassionate,
slow to anger and abounding in love,
and he relents from sending calamity.

Joel 2:12-13

Grace Is the Undeserved Favour of God[42]

Grace is the undeserved favour of God.
It can't be earned,
it is a gift given by the Father through his Son.

However, cheap grace is…

the grace we bestow on ourselves.
It is the preaching of forgiveness without repentance.
It is baptism without church discipline,
release from guilt without personal confession.
It is grace without discipleship.
It is grace without the cross,
grace without the living, incarnate Christ.

Costly grace is life-changing…

---

[42] Inspired by reading Dietrich Bonhoeffer's *The Cost of Discipleship*.

It is the treasure hidden in a field.[43]
It is the pearl of great price.[44]
It is the kingly rule of Christ.
Costly grace loathes sin.
It is the call to follow Christ,
to renounce self,
to submit to his yoke.[45]
Costly grace is not self-bestowed;
it is the call to partake in his suffering,
by way of the cross.[46]

---

[43] Matthew 13:44
[44] Matthew 13:45-46
[45] Matthew 11:28-29
[46] Matthew 16:24-25

Long Ago the Prophets Foretold

Long ago the prophets foretold
of a child who would become a King.
Israel's promised Messiah of old,
God's gift of grace, to all we sing.

God's love is shown to you and me,
through the man who became Israel's King,
teaching us what life should really be.
Our complete lives to you we bring.

Israel killed God's Son, their King,
who was crucified for all to see,
taking onto himself our sin
so we can be blameless and free –

sinners freed by God's good grace,
his Spirit giving new life, new birth.
Selfishness and pride have no place
in God's Kingdom here on earth.

Heavenly Father, Forgive Us, We Pray[47]

Heavenly Father, forgive us, we pray
for being selfish in your world today.
You have given us the run of the land
to sow and harvest with your helping hand.
You gently instruct us to watch and tend
but we vandalise, abuse and offend
your world, our neighbour and our Creator,
saddening your Son, mankind's Saviour.

We have taken your world for granted
and have spoilt what you have created.
We have failed to share our wealth fairly
and been uncaring and unfriendly.
The world's people cry in hopeless despair
at mankind's inability to share.
Heavenly Father, forgive us, we pray
for being selfish in your world today.

---

[47] This poem was written while the civil war raged in Syria causing a refugee crisis in Europe. North Korea was conducting their missile and nuclear tests destabilising the region. A garment factory in Bangladesh collapsed killing over a thousand people and injuring many thousands more, begging the question, where do we source our clothes from and are we giving these people a safe place to work and a fair wage?

Thank you that you're greater than our meanness
and much stronger than our destructiveness,
giving us a fresh start, a new beginning,
a second chance, a new way of living.
Our only hope rests in Jesus Christ your Son;
by his death and new life, the battle's won.
He alone gives us the seeds of faith and love,
a new life by God's Spirit from above.

Our only hope rests in Jesus Christ your Son.
By his death and new life, the battle's won.
He alone gives us the seeds of faith and love,
a new life by God's Spirit from above.

Christ, the Eternal Light Who Guides Our Way

Christ, the eternal light who guides our way;
while darkness abounds, he brightens our day.
Worry he dismisses, hope he imparts,
healing he brings, giving peace to our hearts.

Christ, the eternal light, giver of life.
Nations rebel in bitterness and strife.
Our sin enslaves, his grace releases,
banishing fear, our faith he increases.

Fill us with God's Holy Fire
that we may fulfil his heart's desire:
reflecting Christ's light to every nation
that all may see his healing salvation.

Christ, the eternal light, Saviour of all,
help us respond in faith to your call:
sharing your gospel to those who seek,
guiding the lost, encouraging the weak.

Christ, the eternal light, Lord of our soul,
help us aim towards your kingdom goal
of knowing God, empowered from above,
obeying his law, the greatest being love.

Fill us with God's Holy Fire
that we may fulfil his heart's desire:
reflecting Christ's light to every nation
that all may see his healing salvation.

Love Is…

Love is…
what God did in sending his Son
to be our substitute on the cross.

Love is…
what we do when we keep Christ's commands.

Love is…
sharing with our brethren in need.

Love is…
treating each other with kindness.

Love is…
treating each other with patience.

Love is…
God chastising the rebellious saint.

Love is…
welcoming the prodigal son,
when he sees his wickedness
and, full of sorrow, heads for home.

So Wide, So Deep Is Your Love for Us

So wide, so deep is your love for us,
you sent your perfect Son to us.
We nailed him to a cross.
Then we see and understand your love
and from our hearts we cry, 'Sorry,
O Lord, forgive and rescue us.'

Your love is like a precious stone,
immensely beautiful, flawless and strong.
Our love is like fragile glass,
imperfect, weak and prone to shatter.
Though our love is hurt by sin,
you still reveal perfect love through him.

We love because he first loved us.
His love drives away our fear.
Fear has to do with punishment.
Hate is incompatible with love.
If we hate, we're fooling ourselves
and his love is not within us.

When we face unprovoked anger,
help us not hit back, but to love,
to show that same self-giving love
your Son displayed on the cross.
His love broke the cycle of hate.
His love, your love, conquers all.

When we face hopeless poverty,
when we see the sick and hungry,
help us share your love.
When we see the homeless stranger,
when we face a lonely neighbour,
help us share your love.

Your love is kind and generous.
You love the unlovable.
Likewise, show us how to love
those we find difficult to love.
Your love always protects,
never gives up, always hopes.

When we're tempted, show us the way
so we won't give in to selfish sin.
Help us depend on you, O Lord,
for your love works best when we're weak.
And as you forgive our many sins,
help us forgive those who wrong us.

Help us be clothed with humility.
Help us be filled with inner peace.
Help us be empowered to face life.
For your inner voice calls us to go
and to tell others about your love –
your transforming, life-changing love.

God Is...

God is...

a God of love;
however,
he is holy, he loathes sin.
But through his living
and incarnate Son,
he can save us,
forgive us
and change us,
from vessels of immoral, shameful use[48]
to vessels holy and clean.

Whoever does not love,[49]
does not know God,
because God is...

a God of love.

---

[48] 2 Timothy 2:20-21
[49] 1 John 4:8

Good Friday

'He himself bore our sins' in his body on the cross, so that we might die to sins and live for righteousness; 'by his wounds you have been healed.'

1 Peter 2:24

Good Friday

CONTINUITY ANNOUNCER

> *Jesus and his disciples had spent Thursday evening eating the Passover meal together in the upper room of a friend's house in Jerusalem. Judas had left them, part way through the meal, to betray Jesus to the temple authorities.*
>
> *Leaving the house they walked quietly through the lower part of the city to the Garden of Gethsemane, situated to the east of the temple, on the western slopes of the Mount of Olives. They were in a sombre mood as they approached the moonlit olive grove to find a place to pray.*

NARRATOR 1

> Jesus could feel the cold night air
> clinging to his face,
> as he and the eleven made their way
> to a quiet, sheltered place.
>
> His heart was heavy with a burden
> he could never share,
> of mankind's wickedness
> he alone could bear.

JESUS [WHISPER]

> 'Wait here,'

NARRATOR 2

> whispered Jesus,
> taking Peter, James and John to pray,
> to spend time with his Father
> until the break of day.
>
> Out of reach of his three friends
> he fell face down to the ground.
>
> Praying:

JESUS [FULL OF FEELING]

> 'Oh Father!
> Can some other way be found?'

NARRATOR 1

> Returning to his sleeping friends
> unaware of the trial he faced,
> to die; God's loving sacrifice
> for the human race.
>
> Praying more fervently:

JESUS

> 'Father,
>   let this horror pass me by,'

NARRATOR 1

> his feverish brow glistening
> in the cold moonlit sky.

NARRATOR 2

> Three times he caught them sleeping,
> unaware of the pain he bore:
> the vision of his separation
> from the Father he adored.
>
> Turning his face to the cross,
> the nightmare had begun:
> his betrayer close at hand;
> the sacrifice of God's own Son.

NARRATOR 1

> Jesus could see torches flickering
> as the mob burst through the trees.

JESUS

> 'Whom do you seek?'

NARRATOR 2 [SHOUT]

> 'Jesus!'

JESUS

> 'I am he!'

NARRATOR 1

> The crowd fell to their knees.
>
> They watched in silence
> as Judas
> kissed Jesus on the cheek.
> The prearranged signal:

NARRATOR 2

> 'That's the man,
> whom Caiaphas seeks!'

NARRATOR 1

> The mob surged forward;
> Peter drew his sword
> swinging wildly left then right
> to save his Master and his Lord.

NARRATOR 2

> Striking Caiaphas' servant,
> blood poured from his severed ear.
> Jesus knelt down and healed him,
> the crowd trembling with fear.

NARRATOR 1

> Jesus firmly told Peter:

JESUS [WITH A COMMANDING VOICE]

> 'Put your sword away!
> Shall I not drink this bitter cup
> my Father has passed my way?'

CONTINUITY ANNOUNCER

> *Jesus, now bound like a common criminal, stood alone in the High Priest Caiaphas' palace. All the disciples had fled and only Peter remained standing in the palace courtyard. Even Peter would shortly deny that he ever*

knew Jesus. It was still night-time and a court had been hastily convened to try him.

NARRATOR 1

> The party brought Jesus to the council.
> A show trial took place.

NARRATOR 2 [SNEERING]

> 'Tell us, are you the Christ?'

NARRATOR 1

> All eyes staring intently at his face.

JESUS

> 'It is as you say,'

NARRATOR 1

> Jesus answered,
> knowing he would die.

NARRATOR 2

> The high priest tore his clothes:
> 'This is blasphemy and a lie.'

ALL [BANGING ON A TABLE]

> 'Death! Death!'

NARRATOR 1

> the court all shouted.
> An official struck Jesus on his face.

Bound and led forth from the court,
God's substitute for the human race.

NARRATOR 2

Cross-examined by Pontius Pilate,
no wrong could be found;
his life perfect, his deeds faultless,
his teaching morally sound.

NARRATOR 1

Now early Friday morning
a riotous mob gathered outside.

Shouting:

ALL [SHOUTING]

'Release Barabbas;
Jesus crucify, crucify!'

NARRATOR 2

Afraid, Pilate washed his hands
saying:

NARRATOR 1

'I'm innocent of this man's blood!'

NARRATOR 2

Soldiers mocked him, they flogged him,
his body cut and caked in blood.

Narrator 1

> Through the streets Jesus staggered
> carrying a cross hewn from a tree.
> A symbol of his pain, his suffering,
> his death,

All

> of hope for you and for me.

Continuity Announcer

> *As part of their sentence the condemned prisoner had to carry a heavy wooden cross to the place of execution. Under an armed escort Jesus dragged his cross through the western part of the city. He stumbled and fell, weakened from the brutal flogging he had received earlier in the day. One of the soldiers forced a member of the crowd to carry his cross.*
>
> *Arriving at the place of execution, on a hill outside Jerusalem, Jesus was stripped naked, tied and nailed to his cross which was then hoisted upright into a readymade hole in the ground. Two other criminals were already nailed to their crosses, one on either side of Jesus. The place reeked with the stench of death.*
>
> *Above Jesus' head a notice was fixed saying 'THIS IS JESUS, THE KING OF THE JEWS'.*
>
> *The kingdom Jesus spoke of was never a kingdom to be established and maintained by military force. God's kingdom would come about by way of his self-giving love; his death on a hill outside Jerusalem. He is the light*

on the hill shining into the darkest corners of the world. His loving sacrifice took on the evil of the world, the hatred and cruelty, the gratuitous violence and torture that disfigures God's world. His enthronement will bring healing, forgiveness and hope to countless millions of people in his world.

A centurion keeping watch over Jesus praised God and said, 'Surely he was the Son of God.'

Easter

For the message of the cross is foolishness to those who are perishing, but to us who are being saved it is the power of God.

1 Corinthians 1:18

Despised, Rejected, Nailed to a Cross Was He[50]

Despised, rejected,[51] nailed to a cross was he.
Despised, rejected, nailed to a cross was he.
God's only Son dying for me,
arms outstretched, hands impaled,
hanging there in pain;
in the world's eyes he had failed.

Betrayed by a kiss he hung naked and cold
between two criminals weary and old.
His body pierced, his blood flowing out,
from his lips he uttered a piercing shout:
'My God, my God, have you deserted me?'
Some thought he called Elijah and waited to see
whether he'd come down from the cross.
Instead, he died; the earth trembled at the loss.

His broken body all stiff and cold.
Naked, his clothes divided and sold.
Lowered from the cross, into his friends' waiting arms,
revealing the wounds in his feet and his palms.
Wrapped in linen they laid him in a tomb,
while his disciples, scared, hid in a room –
fearful that they will be next to be caught,
forgetting the three years he had taught.

---

[50] This poem has been performed as a drama.
[51] Isaiah 53

Early Sunday morning there was a knock at the door.
Mary and her friends stood and told what they saw.
His disciples didn't believe the words they had said,
that the tomb was empty, he had risen from the dead.
Later that same day, still hiding in a room,
asking, 'Who stole his body from the tomb?'
Jesus appeared saying, 'Touch me and see!
I am alive, death has no power over me!'

The same is true of those who trust him today.
He died for our sins; the full price he did pay.
With joy in our hearts let us praise his holy name,
who took on himself humanity's sin and shame.

Despised, rejected, nailed to a cross was he.
Despised, rejected, nailed to a cross for me,
nailed to a cross for me,
nailed to a cross for me.
Open your eyes and see;
look at this cross, blood-stained,
his tomb empty; a new life,
a new hope, for you and for me.

I Gaze upon His Cross, Love Poured Out for Me

I gaze upon his cross, love poured out for me,
pure, self-giving love so flawless and free.[52]
Such love compels me to confess my sin,
letting God's Spirit transform me within.

By his sacrifice I have been set free![53]
My sins he forgave; they've no hold on me.
I've been pardoned, I'm guilty no more,[54]
accepted by faith, not works of the law.[55]

By faith in God's Son my friendship's restored;
I'm free to worship my Saviour, my Lord –
refined by God's Spirit, his power in me,[56]
a new creation for the world to see.[57]

Reborn by God's Spirit, a new life I lead,
adopted by God, his Kingdom seed,[58]
to be planted, to grow, in his Son's name,
producing good fruit for God to reclaim.

[52] John 13:1-17
[53] Romans 6:6-7; Galatians 5:1
[54] Hebrews 8:12
[55] Romans 3:28; Galatians 2:16
[56] Malachi 2:17-3:6
[57] 2 Corinthians 5:17
[58] Ephesians 1:5

Through God's mercy his love is secured;
who call on his name, salvation assured.[59]
Help me obey, empowered from above,
to share his Good News with joy and with love.

I gaze upon his cross, love poured out for me,
pure, self-giving love so flawless and free.
Such love compels me to confess my sin,
letting God's Spirit transform me within.

[59] Romans 8:38-39

Pentecost

When the day of Pentecost came, they were all together in one place. Suddenly a sound like the blowing of a violent wind came from heaven and filled the whole house where they were sitting. They saw what seemed to be tongues of fire that separated and came to rest on each of them. All of them were filled with the Holy Spirit and began to speak in other tongues as the Spirit enabled them.

Acts 2:1-4

Devoted In Prayer

Devoted in prayer,
one hundred and twenty followers,
disciples of Jesus,
eagerly await the divine promise of God's seal,
the Holy Spirit.[60]

Seven weeks had passed
since his resurrection.
Ten days had elapsed since his ascension –
ascending to his holy Father,
Israel's God,
our Father in heaven.

I, one of his followers,
stand praying, praising God.
The air's heavy with excitement
that something incredible is about to happen.
A sense of dread overpowers me
as I feel the presence of God.

Lamps flicker, I hear a noise:
a sound of rushing wind.
In the darkness I see flames,
faint tongues of fire,
falling upon each of us.
I feel the warmth of God's searching gaze,
his holiness from above.

---

[60] Joel 2:28-29; Acts 2:1-13

My heart is racing, pulsating,
sensing God in a new way;
Experiencing his cleansing,
God's holy fire,
exposing, devouring my sin.
His love overpowers me, drives me,
to tell others his Good News.

I run from the darkened room
into a crowded street,
people staring as I praise God
using strange, foreign words.
Medes, Parthians are amazed,
hearing God's message spoken in their own language.

Crowds gather,
puzzled, confused,
hearing uneducated men and women

proclaiming Christ's death,
his resurrection.
Repentance,
sins forgiven!
Redemption!
Salvation!
Everlasting peace!
A new beginning!

Holy Spirit

Do you not know that your bodies are temples of the Holy Spirit, who is in you, whom you have received from God? You are not your own; you were bought at a price. Therefore, honour God with your bodies.

1 Corinthians 6:19-20

O Life-giving Spirit

O life-giving Spirit, O life-giving Spirit,
holy God of wind and fire,
O life-changing Spirit, O life-changing Spirit,
fill our hearts with loving service;
producing fruit is God's desire.

Guide us, bring us closer to God's Son;
assure us of what he has done.
Help us trust the promise of his word,
to ask, believing he has heard.

O life-giving Spirit, O life-giving Spirit,
bringer of gifts to a poor church,
O life-changing Spirit, O life-changing Spirit,
help us use the gifts you've given,
to draw and inspire those who search.

Guide us, bring us closer to God's Son;
assure us of what he has done.
Help us trust the promise of his word,
to ask, believing he has heard.

Holy Spirit, Come Blow on Us

Holy Spirit, come blow on us;
renew us, unite us, in a bond of love.
Remove the divisions within your church
that the world may see your love
and obey our Father above.

Lord, come, renew your troubled church,
remove our apathy and fear.
Open our eyes, unblock our ears,
that we, your church, may see and hear
your message of God's saving love;
and, filled with God's Spirit, go forth and tell
this message of hope to a dying world
whose people dwell in darkness and sin,
who need your healing within.

Holy Spirit, come blow on us;
renew us, unite us, in a bond of love.
Remove the divisions within your church
that the world may see your love
and obey our Father above.

Lord, come, renew your troubled church,
rebuild the faith we have in you.
May our doors be open to God's Spirit,[61]
and lead our hearts to worship you,
and lead our hearts to worship you!
May we reflect your light to the world,[62]
a world in rebellion against God
whose people cry in hopeless despair
at man's refusal to care.

Holy Spirit, come blow on us;
renew us, unite us, in a bond of love.
Remove the divisions within your church
that the world may see your love
and obey our Father above.

Lord, come, renew your troubled church,
restore the love we had for you.[63]
May God's Spirit cleanse and renew us
that we may serve and honour you,
that we may serve and honour you!
And may your church be a refuge of peace –
a place where we are encouraged to pray,
like a bride prepared and ready,[64]
awaiting her wedding day.[65]

---

[61] Revelation 3:20
[62] Matthew 5:14
[63] Revelation 2:4
[64] Ephesians 5:23-32
[65] Matthew 25:1-13

*Holy Spirit, come blow on us;
renew us, unite us, in a bond of love.
Remove the divisions within your church
that the world may see your love
and obey our Father above.*

O Spirit of the Living God

O Spirit of the living God,
change our selfish hearts of stone.[66]
Remove our conceit, remove our pride
so we may love Father God alone.
O Spirit of the living God,
fall afresh upon us,
fall afresh upon us.

O Spirit of the living God,
unite us with one voice, we plead.
Teach us to love each other
as we go and plant your kingdom seed.
O Spirit of the living God,
fall afresh upon us,
fall afresh upon us.

---

[66] Ezekiel 11:19; 36:26

Jesus

'I give them eternal life, and they shall never perish; no one will snatch them out of my hand. My Father, who has given them to me, is greater than all; no one can snatch them out of my Father's hand. I and the Father are one.'

John 10:28-30

Jesus, Jesus, I Hear Your Voice

Jesus, Jesus I hear your voice
saying, 'Come, follow me. Rejoice! Rejoice!'

Search my heart; remove all sin;
create a Christ-centred love within.
Holiness I should desire;
pour out on me God's holy fire.

Joined to you, God's holy vine,
producing fruit is the Spirit's sign.
Help me, Lord, obey your call
and in your name share God's love to all.

Jesus, Jesus, I hear your voice
saying, 'Come, follow me. Rejoice! Rejoice!'

Jesus Knows Everything About Me

Jesus knows everything about me.
He knows how I feel;
he knows my innermost thoughts.
Even when I want to hide,
he is there,
ready to love and comfort me.
Am I willing to accept his embrace?

Jesus wants every part of me.
Whether I am at home
or at work,
whether I am in church
or walking the dog,
he is interested in everything I do.
Am I willing to accept his embrace?

Jesus wants my mind…
to be transformed,
renewed,
by reading his word,
thinking on it day and night,
feeding, receiving.
Am I willing to accept his embrace?

Jesus wants my voice...
to encourage,
to teach others
to love him;
to praise, to worship
in Spirit and in truth.
Am I willing to accept his embrace?

Jesus wants my hands...
to touch, to comfort,
those in need;
to serve as he served;
to heal as he healed;
to pray as he prayed.
Am I willing to accept his embrace?

Jesus wants my feet...
to step out in faith;
to run, to not count the cost;
to walk the path of holiness;
to stand firm, to tell others
of God's love as he loves me.
Am I willing to accept his embrace?

Jesus wants every part of me.
He wants my whole body:
my mind, my voice,
my hands, my feet.
To be set apart, a living sacrifice –
this is my spiritual worship.
Am I willing to accept his embrace?

Lord, am I willing to accept your embrace?
Reach out to me;
wrap your arms around me.
Comfort me
as I confess my sins to you
and hear your words
of forgiveness: 'Your sins are no more.'

You Are the Potter

You are the potter,
I am the clay.
In your hands you work me day by day;
squeezing out imperfections, fashioning me anew,
creating a new vessel solely useful to you.

You are the potter,
I am the clay.
In your hands you change me as I pray;
strengthening my resolve when I am tempted to fall;
allowing me to share your love, obeying your call.

You are the potter,
I am the clay,
your hands showing me the price you paid –
hands bearing the scars, explaining your death to me,
demonstrating your love that made me blameless and
 free.

You are the potter,
I am the clay,
God's Spirit guiding me in what I say:
sharing the Good News both in words and in deeds,
allowing you to harvest, picking the fertile seeds.

'Turn to Me, Talk to Me and Trust Me,' You Say

'Turn to me, talk to me and trust me,' you say.
Help me rely on God's mercy, I pray.
Forgive my lack of faith, open my eyes to see
God's life-renewing Spirit at work within me.

Purify my life, then I'll bring glory to you
by producing fruit as your servant must do.
Make me holy within,
free my life from all sin.

'Turn to me, talk to me and trust me,' you say.
Guide my thoughts as I live out my day.
May your amazing love be seen in my deeds
as I go and plant your Good News, God's kingdom seeds.

'Turn to me, talk to me and trust me,' you say.
Help me rely on God's mercy, I pray.
Forgive my lack of faith, open my eyes to see
God's life-renewing Spirit at work within me.

Purify my life, then I'll bring glory to you.

Holy Trinity

May the grace of the Lord Jesus Christ, and the love of God, and the fellowship of the Holy Spirit be with you all.

2 Corinthians 13:14

Holy God, Creator and Father

Holy God, Creator and Father,
who sits upon his heavenly throne,
who sent his loving Son to save us;
salvation found in him alone.

God's Son among us, ever caring,
unite and bless your people, we pray.
Help us to be patient, gentle
and loving in what we do and say.

Make us one, by God's Holy Spirit;
change our deceitful hearts of stone.
Remove our conceit, remove our pride,
so we may worship God alone.

O Father, Son and Holy Spirit,
one Holy God, our praise we bring –
one loving God, coeternal.
We bow in homage before our King.

God Beyond Us, We Worship You[67]

God beyond us, we worship you.
Your Spirit, like an eagle, soars[68]
across the earth you lovingly made;
all that we see and hear is yours.
We can't hold you, yet you hold us,
Almighty God, our Saviour King.
You are our rock when in distress;[69]
O loving God, to you we cling.

A Father's love shown through his Son –
salvation found in him alone –
creating life with his Father[70]
who sits upon his heavenly throne;
sent by his Father to live as man,[71]
showing what life should truly be.
He existed before all time;
throughout his life, God's love we see.

---

[67] This poem was a result of me wrestling with the concept of the Holy Trinity! I settled on the idea that the Holy Trinity teaches us about community and family. The poem has also been set to music and used in various church services, the music arranged by my nephew for the piano. The words 'You are our rock when in distress. O loving God, to you we cling' have been particularly meaningful to me in recent years since I was diagnosed with Parkinson's.
[68] Genesis 1:2
[69] Psalm 71:3
[70] John 1:3; Colossians 1:16
[71] John 5:37

Eternal Son of the true God,
healing the sick, the lame and blind;
he bore our sin, he bore our shame,
was crucified for all mankind.
Dead and buried, he rose to life,
paving the way for all who see –
our loving brother alongside us[72]
giving us life and setting us free.

Holy Spirit, we worship you,
Most Holy God of wind and fire,[73]
sent by the Father and his Son[74]
to reassure and to inspire,
drawing us all to Abba God,
binding us with cords of love.
He rests on us his holy seal[75]
with cleansing fire from above.

God three-in-one – one family
showing what life should truly be –
created man in his image[76]
to live in peace and harmony.
O Father, Son, Holy Spirit,
one loving God, our praise we bring;
one holy God, coeternal.
Hallelujah to God our King!

---

[72] John 20:17
[73] Acts 2:2-3
[74] John 15:26
[75] Ephesians 1:13
[76] Genesis 1:27

Father, Son, Holy Spirit,
one loving God, our praise we bring;
one holy God, coeternal.
Hallelujah to God our King!

God, the Creator of All We See

God, the Creator of all we see:
the hills, the mountains, the lakes, the sea,
the heavens above, the earth below.
Through God's Son his Father we know.

Death on a cross, salvation is won;
victory supplied by raising his Son.
Trust in his name, his promise is sure!
Death defeated, our hope is secure.

Through God's Son his Father we know.
Reborn by God's Spirit, by faith we can grow,
enabled to worship his Father above,
through his sacrifice revealing God's love.

Praise to the Father, praise to the Son,
praise to the Spirit, our God three-in-one.
We worship with incense, our prayers of love,[77]
with hearts of obedience to our Father above.

---

[77] Revelation 8:4

Holy, Holy, Great and Awesome Is He

Holy, holy, great and awesome is he,
Lord God, one God, one loving family.

Father Creator, we glimpse your beauty
in a setting sun, icy mountain stream.
We sense your power in a lightning flash,
hurricane wind, ocean's roar, thunder crash.

Precious Jesus, we see your body –
pure love poured out for humankind –
nailed to a cross, a blood-stained tree,
tormented, humiliated, for all to see.

Holy Spirit, we see your power
in lives reborn, hearts on fire;
calling our name, a still small voice
comforting, guiding our hearts to rejoice.

Holy, holy, great and awesome is he,
Lord God, one God, one loving family.

Worship

Yours, LORD, is the greatness and the power
and the glory and the majesty and the splendour,
for everything in heaven and earth is yours.
Yours, LORD, is the kingdom;
you are exalted as head over all.

1 Chronicles 29:11

Holy, Holy Is the Lord

Holy, holy is the Lord.
Holy, holy is the Lord.
Salvation, glory,
majesty and power
belong to our God
forever and ever.

Lift up your hands;
give him the glory.
Lift up your hands;
rejoice and praise
to the King of Kings
who reigns forevermore!

Holy, holy is the Lord.
Holy, holy is the Lord.
Salvation, glory,
majesty and power
belong to our God
forever and ever.

Lift up your hands;
give him the glory.
Lift up your hands;
rejoice and praise
to the King of Kings
who reigns forevermore!

Death and New Life

Brothers and sisters, we do not want you to be uninformed about those who sleep in death, so that you do not grieve like the rest of mankind, who have no hope. For we believe that Jesus died and rose again, and so we believe that God will bring with Jesus those who have fallen asleep in him.

1 Thessalonians 4:13-14

He Is Eternal, the First and the Last[78]

He is eternal, the first and the last,[79]
Lord of the future, Lord of the past,
Maker of all time, of all space,[80]
Lord Creator of the human race.

He is the Lamb who suffered and died.
'Father, forgive them!' the Lord he cried,[81]
hanging on a cross made from a tree,
forgiving our sin, setting us free.[82]

'Hallelujah!'
the heavenly host cry,
to the Lamb of God
who was tortured and slain.[83]
'Hallelujah!'
his people reply,
to the One who carried
our sin and our shame.

---

[78] The words to this poem came to me while my father lay dying from dementia; he too suffered from Parkinson's. I used it as a prayer. The final verse reminds us of the hope we have in Jesus that God's world will be renewed and death defeated by his risen might.
[79] Revelation 22:13
[80] John 1:3
[81] Luke 23:34
[82] Colossians 2:13-14
[83] Revelation 5:12

He frees the sinner by his grace;[84]
envy and pride have no place
in his kingdom here on earth –
giver of life, a new rebirth.[85]

He is the Saviour of mankind,
the eternal peace to those who find
heaven's Lamb, the bringer of life,
who rescues us from evil and strife.

'Hallelujah!'
the heavenly host cry,
to the Lamb of God
who was tortured and slain.
'Hallelujah!'
his people reply,
to the One who carried
our sin and our shame.

He frees the world from the curse of sin;
heaven and earth renewed by him.
The dead will rise, new life in Christ,[86]
death defeated by his risen might.[87]

---

[84] Ephesians 2:8
[85] John 3:3
[86] 1 Thessalonians 4:16
[87] 2 Timothy 1:10

'Hallelujah!'
the heavenly host cry,
to the Lamb of God,
who was tortured and slain.
'Hallelujah!'
his people reply,
to the One who carried
our sin and our shame.

We Mourn the Passing of Those We Love[88]

We mourn the passing of those we love,
shedding a tear for those who sleep,
knowing that there's hope in Christ above,[89]
in whose arms they find rest and peace.

Death defeated by Christ's risen might,[90]
he paved the way for those who believe;
guiding the saints by his holy light,
who await creation's redemption.[91]

Heaven and earth renewed as one[92]
in a burst of creative power[93]
by God the Father and his Son,
restoring a world, free from all sin.

A world brimming with God's goodness,
a place of wonderful beauty,
a home filled with God's holiness,
where those washed in Christ's blood can dwell.[94]

---

[88] This poem was written after hearing the passing away of my Christian friend Paul. His wife Beverly included it in the book of condolence. The Christian death is not the end but just the beginning. I can say this with certainty because of the resurrection of our Lord, Jesus Christ. For forty days he showed himself to his disciples both in Jerusalem and Galilee. He ate fish with them to show that he was a physical human being. He invited Thomas to touch his wounds. He also revealed himself to the Apostle Paul, who, before his conversion, persecuted the Christian believers and was complicit in the stoning of Stephen (Acts 7:60).
[89] 1 Thessalonians 4:13-14
[90] 2 Timothy 1:10
[91] Romans 8:18-22
[92] Revelation 21:1
[93] 1 Corinthians 15:52
[94] Colossians 1:20-22; Hebrews 13:12

A world as God meant it to be:
a place where there's no suffering and death,[95]
a home to live for eternity;
an exciting, corporeal, renewed earth.

---

[95] Revelation 21:4

My Faith Journey

When at the age of nineteen I arrived at Sheffield University for Freshers' Week, I had no idea that my life was about to change. It all began when a friend from school invited me to a coffee evening during that week. Everyone was very friendly, and someone stood up and described how they had become a Christian. I could relate to their story. To me, God was remote and I certainly didn't have a relationship with Jesus Christ.

My parents weren't churchgoers. My father was a lapsed Roman Catholic and my mother a lapsed Methodist. As young children my brother and I were sent to a local Congregational church, a couple of doors away from where we lived in Chester, but we stopped going in our early teens. In the lower sixth I was invited to a meeting in Liverpool where a Romanian pastor, Richard Wurmbrand, gave a talk about his work behind the Iron Curtain. He and his wife smuggled bibles into Romania and Russia, and told amazing stories of believers who were willing to suffer persecution and die for their Christian faith. They too had suffered imprisonment and torture for their faith. In the summer of 1973, I volunteered to help with the Chester Festival. I met an Augustine monk who did amazing sculptures, in wood and stone, depicting Jesus Christ's death on the cross. The exhibition was held in St Werburgh's Crypt, under the cathedral. I can recall sitting there and asking God what it all meant as I thumbed through a 1662 Book of Common Prayer!

So it all fell into place when I was invited to that coffee evening in Sheffield. I knelt at my bedside, that evening in September, confessing my sins and inviting Jesus into my life –

the first faltering steps of my newfound faith. I say 'faltering' as there were many activities on offer and being invited to a Bible study wasn't one of them! However, over the Christmas holiday my attitude changed, and in January I started Bible study. I found out later that my name was on the national prayer diary of the Navigators[96]. I was later baptised at a Baptist church in Sheffield in spring 1974.

One of the highlights of my time with the Navigators was an international conference at Essen, Germany in 1977. Christians across Europe were invited to the conference. At one of the meetings, we were invited to renew our calling, and my RSV bible is marked with 'ECDM Easter 1977' at the place where Jesus commands his disciples to go and make disciples and promises that he will be with them always (Matthew 28:19-20).

I met my wife in my final year. Pam was studying an MSc in Information Science while I was finishing my MA in Architecture. We were married in 1980 and moved to Oldham, Greater Manchester. Newly qualified as an architect, I worked for a practice in Oldham and British Nuclear Fuels working on their new headquarters at Risley, Warrington. After two years I was transferred to Sellafield, Cumbria, living at St Bees, a seaside village and a wonderful place to start a family. Our two sons were born in Cumbria. For those of you who are interested in fell walking, St Bees is famous for Wainwright's coast to coast walk to Robinhood's Bay, on the east coast, a small fishing village close to Whitby. We lived in a sandstone cottage in the middle of St Bees and there we got involved with the Priory Church and led the Young Christians' Group (fifteen or so

---

[96] See footnote 1, p.vii.

teenagers) meeting in our home. We also went to an ecumenical house-group meeting in the village; there were members from a house church, Assembles of God, Methodist and Anglican. We studied the Bible together and enjoyed each other's fellowship.

When our youngest son was eight weeks old, we moved to East Ardsley, Wakefield. We eventually settled into an Anglican church at South Ossett where we met Paul and Beverly. Their children are a similar age to ours. Pam met Beverly at the church mother and toddler group. Paul and I met in our lunchtime at Headingley, Leeds where we both worked; we had a walk and prayed together. Paul had been involved with the Navigators at Leeds University.

Eventually I was promoted and transferred to Salford, Manchester, but found the partner difficult to work with and I couldn't face the driving to Manchester each day. I was successful in securing another job in Leeds but the project I was working on was shelved and I found myself out of work. The recession hit the building industry very hard and I was unemployed for a year. In that time, I entered a couple of architectural competitions to keep my portfolio fresh, and volunteered working in a Christian bookshop in Wakefield.

Eventually I secured a six-month contract with a practice in Scarborough and then secured a permanent position working for a practice in Colwyn Bay, North Wales. On my first day at work, one of the partners stormed out of the office, warning me to bide my time before moving my family to North Wales. The first two years were idyllic, and as a reward I was given the office runabout to help me in travelling home on a Friday evening and travelling back on a Sunday evening. I saw people come and go. A friend of mine from the same practice in Leeds, who was made redundant, on my recommendation got a job with the practice but found the partner in charge very difficult to work with and resigned. My third year was awful. The partner in charge was trying to get me sacked so he could give my job to one of his friends. I found this out from the practice secretary. He also instructed his staff not to talk to me; needless to say, they didn't obey him. Friends at my church in South Ossett were praying for me. Through my time in Colwyn Bay, I kept a prayer diary as a way of encouraging myself. I felt I was trapped in a long tunnel with little prospect of escape.

My friend Paul, in South Ossett, saw an advert for a job in a Christian magazine. The office was located in central Manchester. A day or so later I met David, a director of an advertising company who was working on a project I was involved with in Bangor. We got talking and I found that he was a Christian. His father was one of the directors of the company Paul had seen advertising for an architect. I applied for the job and stayed with the company for nearly twenty-five years, working mainly on church projects. My MA dissertation was on *The Design and Use of Multipurpose Church Centres,* and little did I know that the rest of my architectural career would be spent designing similar churches. Quite a lot of my poetry-writing on trusting God coincided with my time spent in Colwyn Bay.

My call to preach occurred when my wife and I decided that we should try to support a local church. Pam had got friendly with one of the teachers at the local primary school at East Ardsley. At the time she was a teaching assistant at the school. We were invited to the church and found it extremely friendly. In 2003 I started my studying to become a Local Preacher and initially got through the first couple of modules quite quickly. However, we started having trouble with my youngest son, and my mother started with Alzheimer's disease which involved regular trips to Chester. This and commuting to Manchester each day meant I was struggling with my studying. My father was also diagnosed with Parkinson's disease. We eventually got both parents into the same care home.

I completed my studying and was admitted and recognised as a Local Preacher in the Methodist Church in June 2009.

At my mum's funeral in December 2011 (I did the eulogy) I reminisced how my mum rang Pam and I, telling us that she had become a Christian. I jokingly replied I would give her a couple of months, reminding her of the time when she had said that to me way back in 1973! My sister and her husband became Christians around the same time as my mum.

I was diagnosed with Parkinson's disease in October 2017 which came as a bit of a shock. Thankfully the uncontrolled shaking appears to be affecting my right hand only and not my walking or speech. Unfortunately, my ability to draw, to write and to play my guitar has been affected. However, I can type my poetry and still preach, although the shaking intensifies when I get excited or under stress. At times this can be quite amusing when I am watching an exciting film! The following year I was diagnosed with bladder cancer which required BCG treatment. The tumour was fortunately found at an early stage, as this type of cancer can be very aggressive. I have six-monthly check-ups to see that the cancer has not returned.

I can only praise God that I have lived to see both my grandsons, with a third one on the way.

The Covid pandemic was a testing time for us all. During the first lockdown, in April 2020, Pam and I had to make the decision whether to look after our two-year-old grandson, as his mum was a key worker. Joel stayed with us for over two months. We went on long walks, where he was carried on Grandad's back, and he played in our lovely garden (Pam and I love gardening). It was lovely to see the world through his eyes. The last night of his stay, he wanted to sleep in a tent with his granddad.

I mentioned the Congregational church I went to as young child. I started to attend the church again in early 1973 and helped out with the Sunday school. One of the topics was the life of Dietrich Bonhoeffer, a Lutheran pastor who was imprisoned and executed by the Nazis in 1945 – like Richard Wurmbrand, who twenty years later was willing to suffer imprisonment and torture for his faith. I began to ask God why such people were willing to die. People rarely die for half-hearted belief. 'Costly grace is not self-bestowed. It is the call to partake in his suffering, by way of the cross.'[97] C.S. Lewis wrote, 'Christ says, "Give me all. I don't want so much of your time and so much of your money and so much of your work: I want you. I have not come to torment your natural self, but to kill it."'[98] Following Christ is costly.

My story of how I came to faith could have been so different. When I was twelve years old, I lacerated both arms going through a glass door. I was chasing my younger brother around the garden. My left arm still has a nasty four-inch scar. How I managed to miss the artery is a miracle. When I was fifteen years old, I was accidentally knocked off my bicycle while cycling to the train station on the way to school. A bus drove over me. Fortunately, I fell between the wheels, although my bicycle was crushed. As a result of the accident, I have a scar over my right eye. I also fractured one of my vertebrae, spending

---

[97] *The Cost of Discipleship;* Dietrich Bonhoeffer
[98] *Mere Christianity;* C.S. Lewis

a couple of weeks sleeping downstairs on a board until my back healed. I can still see the bus driving over me and what felt like an electric shock as I was dragged along the road. God was looking after me even before I became a Christian.

In my retirement I enjoy cycling and walking the dog. It is as I am walking that some ideas come to mind for my poetry and preaching. My wife and I are also involved with the AWE worship group and Messy Church. We enjoy our cottage holidays, walking in God's 'good' creation, particularly in Norfolk and the Scottish Borders. We also enjoy looking after our grandchildren.

If we knew in advance what our lives would be like, the unexpected twists and turns, we would likely give up. As our lives unfold, trusting God and obeying his voice is quite comforting. It takes away the stress and the uncertainty. There is a verse in the Bible which says a similar thing which I memorised as a young Christian from the Revised Standard Version: 'Have no anxiety about anything, but in everything by prayer and supplication with thanksgiving let your requests be made known to God. And the peace of God, which passes all understanding, will keep your hearts and your minds in Christ Jesus.' (Philippians 4:6-7, RSV).

Ian K. Caveen
Wakefield, UK
May 2022

Similar Books from the Publisher

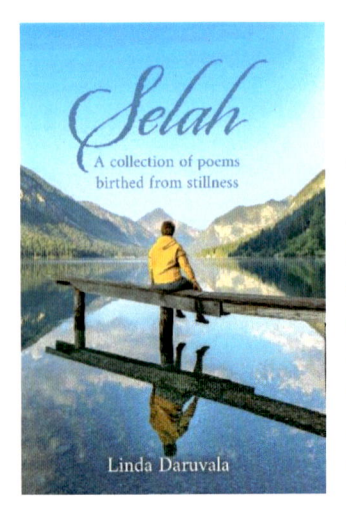

Selah
Linda Daruvala
ISBN 978-1-78815-610-3

This spiritually nourishing collection of poetry was written as Linda Daruvala paused and reflected on Christian retreats and in places of stillness. From poetic paintings of God's creation to a Psalm-like outpouring of her heart to God, Linda echoes the experiences and emotions that are common to many of us in our journey with the Lord.

Faith in His Future
Adele Pilkington
ISBN 978-1-907509-89-6

Adele Pilkington's poems take us on a biblical journey, visiting heroes of the faith and learning from their lives. Each one has a message to share with us today. True heroes do not require great skill or strength, but are those who simply trust in God and act upon His promises.

Books available from all good bookshops and from the publisher: **www.onwardsandupwards.org**